WALKING DEVO

THE DARTMOOR RIVERS

THE
RIVER TEIGN

Richard Easterbrook
&
Geoff Broadhurst

EASTERHURST PUBLICATIONS LTD

Photographs by Richard Easterbrook
Sketches by Geoff Broadhurst

ISBN 0 9538272 2 4
© Richard Easterbrook & Geoff Broadhurst 2005

First published in 2005 by Easterhurst Publications Ltd
11, Warwick Close, Feniton, Devon, EX14 3DT.

Printed and bound in England by
Short Run Press Ltd, Exeter, Devon.

Note:- The information given in this book has been provided in good faith and is intended for general guidance only. Whilst all reasonable efforts have been made to ensure that details were correct at the time of publication, the authors and publisher cannot accept responsibility for any inaccuracies which may result from changes that occur after going to print. It remains the responsibility of any person undertaking outdoor pursuits, to approach them with caution, and, if inexperienced, to do so under proper supervision. The walk described in this book can be strenuous in places and you should therefore ensure that you are fit enough to complete any section that you embark upon, particularly those over open moorland.

Cover Photographs
Front - Spara Bridge, Lower Ashton
Back - Wallabrook Bridge

2

PREFACE

After air and sunlight, water is mankind's most precious commodity. Its presence, be it in the form of ocean, lake, river or garden pond, seems to exert an unfailing magnetism and fascination to all those who venture near it. Devon is fortunate in having more than its fair share of water, with its two coastlines attracting a host of visitors every year. Inland numerous rivers rise, principally from the heights of Dartmoor, Exmoor or the Blackdown Hills, before finding their way to the sea. With few exceptions the rivers complete their journeys at one of Devon's eleven estuaries, more than in any other English County.

Walking is undoubtedly one of the most popular outdoor leisure pursuits in this country, and, by using the vast network of public rights of way, a means of access to the countryside is available that enables it to be enjoyed by all. Additionally, large areas of Dartmoor, with its many antiquities, are accessible to all those who are able to explore on foot. Over the years we have gained much pleasure and satisfaction from walking alongside Devon's rivers, whilst at the same time exploring the varied and delightful countryside through which they flow. The idea for this series of books originated as a result of us deciding to set out to walk as many of Devon's rivers as we could. Although this is the third book in the series it is our first book on one of the numerous rivers that rise on Dartmoor. There are many excellent books, guides and information packs on the subject of Devon's rivers, or parts of rivers, however we could find none that gave a 'walking boots' eye view of what is to be encountered when walking an entire river from source to sea. In this book every stile, gate and footbridge along the way is mentioned, in fact all that you pass by, go through, over, under or across, by walking the described route.

Through this series of books we wish to share with you the immense enjoyment, pleasure and sense of achievement that walking these rivers gave us, and hope that the books will encourage you to embark upon **WALKING DEVON'S RIVERS** yourself.

Richard Easterbrook
&
Geoff Broadhurst

0953827224

ISBN

3

Also available in the series entitled
'WALKING DEVON'S RIVERS'

THE RIVER AXE
ISBN 0 9538272 0 8
THE RIVER OTTER
ISBN 0 9538272 1 6

At the time of going to print the following book,
in the same series, was in the course of preparation

THE RIVER BOVEY and **RIVER LEMON**

For more details e-mail richeasterbrook@aol.com

ACKNOWLEDGEMENTS

This book was made possible with the help of many people. The Authors would like to extend their thanks to staff at Devon County Council's Environment Directorate for their assistance when we needed to check and verify the rights of way information. Thanks are also due to the staff at the County Library in Exeter for their patience and enthusiasm in helping us to obtain useful sources of information.

As with our previous books 'guinea pigs' either volunteered or were press-ganged into carrying out the unenviable task of walking the route using only the directions and sketches given in this book. Our grateful thanks this time go to Sharon Macey, Dave Thomas, Dave Lewis and Ian Yates all of whom, we are pleased to say, arrived at their intended destinations none the worst for their experiences! To those who have also helped but we have not mentioned - thank you.

CONTENTS

PART 1
GENERAL ADVICE FOR WALKERS

EQUIPMENT, SAFETY and COMFORT

The walk involves crossing a variety of terrain, taking in moorland, field, woodland, road and estuary foreshore, and ranges from a few fairly steep sections to the more gentle ramble alongside the estuary itself. Whilst essential for moorland walking, it is also necessary to wear appropriate and comfortable footwear for the other sections of the walk. You should also carry good waterproofs and spare dry clothing, especially when on the moor, as the weather can change quickly and dramatically. For the same reason a compass becomes a necessity as are good maps. We would recommend taking the Ordnance Survey 'Explorer' Maps OL28 (Dartmoor) and 110 (Torquay & Dawlish), as together they cover the entire walk and will assist in identifying features along the route. Finally, a small first aid kit may come in handy.

PUBLIC RIGHTS OF WAY

The Definitive Map

All Public Rights of Way are shown on a 'Definitive Map'. This is the legal record of these Rights of Way for each County. It was produced in England and Wales as a result of the 1949 National Parks and Access to the Countryside Act. Local Authorities are obliged to keep these records up to date to show any legal changes to the network. Each Right of Way has a unique number according to the Parish it is in and the type of Right of Way – i.e. Chudleigh, Footpath 9 or Chagford, Bridleway 2. Ordnance Survey 'Explorer' and 'Landranger' Maps show most public rights of way but will obviously not show any changes made after the maps were published.

The Rights of Way used by the route described in this book were checked against the Definitive Map (Devon) in June 2005.

Types of Rights of Way

Three categories of Public Right of Way exist, which, along with their basic legal definitions, are as follows:-

Footpath (coloured Yellow)
A highway over which the public have a right of way on foot only.

Bridleway (coloured Blue)
A highway over which the public have the right of way on foot, or to ride or lead a horse (or mule or donkey). Pedal cycles are also allowed but cyclists have to give way to pedestrians and riders. There is no right to drive a vehicle.

Byway (coloured Red)
A highway over which the public not only have a right of way as for bridleways but for vehicular use as well.

Permissive Path (coloured Green)
A path over which the right of passage is at the discretion of the landowner and can be withdrawn at anytime.

Access Land
Much of Dartmoor is open access land over which the right of passage is also at the discretion of landowners and, as with Permissive Paths, can be withdrawn at anytime. Such areas of land are clearly defined on OS 'Explorer' Maps

The Use of Public Rights of Way

A Right of Way is what it implies – a right of passage over the ground. You do not have the right to roam at will or use the ground for any other purpose. Although Right of Ways should be kept open and unobstructed you should bear in mind that landowners are not obliged to provide a good surface or signpost the route across their land. You are required to keep to the correct line at all times, but this is not always possible, or it is sometimes impractical to do so. For example, you may come across a deliberate illegal obstruction such as a barbed wire fence, or it may be simply a fallen tree or branch. In either case, you are allowed to remove the obstacle sufficiently to get past or you may take a short alternative route around it. You are also permitted to take a short detour, (keeping close to a field boundary wherever possible) to overcome a broken stile or footbridge for example.

THE COUNTRY CODE

Remember that by using the paths properly and following the Country Code, you are much less likely to come across any problems.

- Enjoy the countryside and respect its life and work.
- Guard against all risk of fire
- Fasten all gates
- Keep your dogs under close control, and always on a lead when there is livestock around
- Keep to the public paths
- Use gates and stiles to cross fences, hedges and walls
- Leave livestock, crops and machinery alone
- Take your litter home
- Help to keep all water clean
- Take special care on country roads - face oncoming traffic
- Protect wildlife, plants and trees

AND MOST IMPORTANT OF ALL

- **TAKE NOTHING**   -   but photographs and memories
- **LEAVE NOTHING**   -   but footprints

PART 2
THE ROUTE

THE COURSE OF THE RIVER TEIGN

Total length	37.5 miles from (North) Teign Head
Source	North Teign - Grid Reference SX 614840
	South Teign - Grid Reference SX 643827
Finish	The Ness, Shaldon - Grid Reference SX 941721
Height at Source	North Teign - 524 metres (1720 feet)
	South Teign - 455 metres (1493 feet)
Main Tributaries	Walla Brook (N.Teign) and Rivers Bovey and Lemon

The Teign starts life as two feeder rivers both rising on northern Dartmoor. The **North Teign** is the longer of the two and rises to the west of **Quintin's Man.** Two miles to the south-east the **South Teign** rises to the east of the **Grey Wethers** stone circles. After starting off in a south-easterly direction the North Teign swings round to follow a generally north-easterly course as it skirts the north-western fringes of Fernworthy Forest. After being joined by the Walla Brook, it then flows east through a steeply wooded valley beneath Gidleigh Tor before turning to the south to reach **Leigh Bridge,** where it is joined by the South Teign. It is from this confluence, having dropped its 'North' and 'South' prefixes, that the Teign begins its remaining thirty mile journey to the sea. Flowing in an easterly direction the river passes to the north of the small market town of **Chagford,** a Stannary town, and then on under Rushford Bridge. It continues eastwards through the beautiful Teign Gorge passing by Castle Drogo perched high on the northern slopes. After passing the renowned beauty spot of **Fingle Bridge** the river continues eastwards, still flanked by the steeply wooded slopes that typify this part of its journey. Only after reaching **Steps Bridge** does the river enter open countryside again, passing to the south of the village of **Dunsford.** At this point the river bends to take a south-easterly course as far as **Bridford Mills** after which it runs almost due south. It has now entered an area rich in mining history with remains of former quarries much in evidence. Passing the villages of **Bridford** and **Christow** to the east, and **Doddiscombsleigh** to the west, the Teign is hugged by the B3193 road on its western bank all the way towards Chudleigh Bridge, south-west of **Chudleigh.** The river bisects the town and its neighbour, **Chudleigh Knighton,** before flowing south-east to meet up with its largest tributary, the River Bovey. Flowing through an area known as the Bovey Basin, an area rich in Ball Clay, the Teign soon reaches the large market town of **Newton Abbot** which it passes to the north-east, and where it is joined by the River Lemon. After flowing under the viaduct carrying the A380 its broad estuary is reached. The Teign estuary is four miles in length and runs due east to the sea. The village of **Bishopsteignton** nestles on the estuary's northern shoreline, whilst the character villages of **Coombeinteignhead** and **Stokeinteignhead** lie to the south. Near the end of its journey one last bridge spans the Teign. Shaldon Bridge connects **Shaldon** on the southern side with the larger resort of **Teignmouth** on the northern side. The sound of waves breaking at the foot of **The Ness** mark the end of this river's delightful and varied thirty seven mile journey.

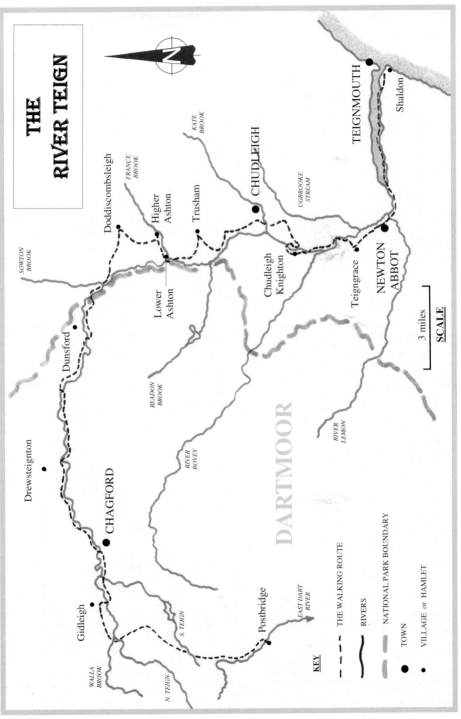

THE RIVER TEIGN

TEIGNMOUTH

Shaldon

CHUDLEIGH

KATE BROOK

Doddiscombsleigh

FRANCE BROOK

Higher Ashton

Trusham

UGBROOKE STREAM

NEWTON ABBOT

Chudleigh Knighton

Teigngrace

SOWTON BROOK

Lower Ashton

Dunsford

3 miles

SCALE

BEADON BROOK

Drewsteignton

RIVER BOVEY

RIVER LEMON

CHAGFORD

DARTMOOR

Gidleigh

S. TEIGN

Postbridge

EAST DART RIVER

WALLA BROOK

N. TEIGN

THE WALKING ROUTE

RIVERS

NATIONAL PARK BOUNDARY

● TOWN

• VILLAGE or HAMLET

KEY

9

PART 3
THE WALK

WALK DETAILS

Total length	44.41 miles
Start	Postbridge Car Park - Grid Reference SX 647788
Finish	The Ness (Shaldon) - Grid Reference SX 941720
Highest point reached	Grey Wethers at 480 metres (1,574 feet) - SX 638 832
Towns and Villages	Postbridge, Chagford, Dunsford, Doddiscombsleigh,
on the route	Ashton, Trusham, (Chudleigh), Chudleigh Knighton,
	Newton Abbot, Shaldon and Teignmouth

The Teign is one of the loveliest rivers that shape Devon's unequalled landscape. The river rises on Dartmoor as two branches, the North and South Teign, which combine as one at Leigh Bridge. Along with its two main tributaries, the Bovey and Lemon, the Teign flows entirely within Devon on its thirty seven mile journey to the sea. After leaving the moors the river passes through wonderfully varied terrain. A steep sided gorge, lush green pastures and mining areas are all traversed before reaching its tidal limits and its broad estuary. The English Channel becomes its ultimate destination. Somewhat rather disappointingly, the derivation of the name 'Teign' simply signifies 'Water'.

WALK DESCRIPTIONS

The walk as described in this book is over forty four miles long. It has been designed as a continuous walk over three or four days but could be done in individual sections over a period of time. The descriptions and accompanying sketches which have been produced are based on a route which has been walked and checked by us many times. We hope that the book will be of use to everyone who enjoys walking and that the descriptions and sketch maps present an accurate and easy to follow guide.

However, the passage of time can introduce changes at the hands of both man and nature; that signpost or stile may no longer be there, or that footbridge washed away. There is also the distinct possibility that a footpath may have become re-routed or even new ones introduced; for example, where a new bridge or road have been constructed or if changes in farming methods have to be accommodated. Most landowners tend to be very co-operative in keeping rights of way clear of obstruction. Indeed, not once during our walking did we come across any blatant obstruction.

The English seasons do of course present their own natural challenges to the walker, from the overgrown grass, nettles and brambles of summer, to the boggy and slippery surfaces in winter. It should be specifically borne in mind that the initial stages of the walk involves walking over open moorland and the inherent dangers associated with walking on such terrain should be heeded. Dartmoor is infamous for its instantly changing weather which can then make walking conditions extremely unpleasant.

Therefore you should make checking the weather forecast your first and utmost priority. The final stage of the walk is along the estuary foreshore and should only be attempted at low tide. Although it should not be necessary to deviate from the described route, any experienced walker armed with the relevant Ordnance Survey map should have no difficulty in finding an alternative route should the need arise.

As far as possible, the walk has been deliberately routed to use only footpaths, bridleways, byways and open access land, but some road walking is inevitable. Where a 'permissive path' has been used it is indicated as such in the walk descriptions. The sketches and descriptions, when read in conjunction with Ordnance Survey maps, should make it possible for you to complete the walk without any problems. Except on the moor the route of the walk is reasonably well signposted and waymarked on the ground, but may not always be straightforward to follow without the aid of this book and appropriate maps.

PLANNING YOUR WALK

General

For those of you who wish to complete the walk with a minimal amount of stops, we would suggest that you make it a four day walk; from Postbridge to Chagford on the first day, Chagford to Steps Bridge (Dunsford) on the second day, Steps Bridge to Chudleigh Knighton on the third day and then the remainder to Shaldon on the fourth day. If however, you wish to spend more time looking around the various places of interest along the way, we would suggest that you do the walk over five or six days to suit your own walking speed and transport arrangements. It should then be possible for you to cover several sections in a day, to include refreshment stops etc, and still have ample time to look around. In either of the above cases, and with the lone walker in mind, we have taken into consideration the availability of car parking and public transport along the way. This ensures that no retracing of steps should be necessary to get back again. Our own preference was to leave a car at the 'finish' of our days walk and then use public transport to get to the 'start'. There are two advantages in doing this; firstly, it acts as a good safeguard should the 'unexpected' happen, such as no bus turning up at the other end; secondly, it gives you the opportunity to ramble without having to keep an 'eye on the clock'.

Accommodation

The three towns along the route, Chagford, Newton Abbot and Teignmouth, have numerous accommodation possibilities and therefore we have not attempted to list them. Any of the local Tourist Information Centres, listed in **Part 4,** will be able to help you to find suitable accommodation in these towns and the surrounding areas.

Public Houses

In **Part 4** we have included a list of Public Houses which are on or within half a mile of the walking route

USING THE SKETCH MAPS AND WALK DESCRIPTIONS

General

The whole walk from Postbridge to Shaldon has been divided into eighteen sections. These have been largely determined by the need to clearly define the route using what we hope are concise, easy to follow notes and sketch maps. As a result sections range from 0.95 mile to 3.95 miles in length, with the actual length of a section being indicated at the head of the page immediately opposite the corresponding sketch map.

Places of Interest and Facilities

Brief descriptive notes on places and points of interest along the way have been included. Facilities available on or near the route have also been indicated, either in the notes themselves, or on the sketch maps. To assist you in planning ahead, particularly when walking the more remote sections, we have indicated distances to the next available facilities.

Transport

Bus Stops and Service Numbers have been shown on the maps where appropriate and afford the opportunity to break your journey if necessary. Because bus services and times are liable to frequent changes, only the current services (at the time of going to print) and their operators have been listed in **Part 4,** along with Train and Taxi operators.

SYMBOLS USED

A ⬤ symbol indicates the start of paragraphs containing the specific walking directions, which are **highlighted in bold text.**

Key to Sketch Map Symbols

FP	Footpath	FB	Footbridge
BW	Bridleway	Wk	Waymark
WC	Public Convenience	PO	Post Office
G	Garage (selling refreshments etc)	LC	Level Crossing
S	Shop (in villages only)	PH	Public House
TIC	Tourist Information Centre	GP	Guide Post
•—•	Gate or Stile	——	Wall (brick, stone or concrete)
][	Bridge	⊔⊔⊔	Fence (wood, iron or wire)
▪▪▪	Railway	aaaa	Hedge or Scrub
(	Public Telephone	⋝⋜	Panoramic View

➡ **Start of Section**   – – – – **The Walking Route**

THE START OF YOUR WALK

Postbridge is situated at the very heart of Dartmoor's National Park thus making it the ideal place for the start of many fine moorland walks including the first two sections described in this book. It is easy to get to by car and is conveniently served by the 'Transmoor' bus link which operates between Exeter and Plymouth. Starting the walk here also provides a relatively accessible means of passing close to the sources of both the South and North Teign Rivers with the added bonus of having to walk alongside part of the East Dart River to do so. Our own preference for covering the moorland sections of the walk without having to retrace our steps, was to leave a car at Chagford and from there catch a bus to Moretonhampstead to arrive in time to connect with a 'Transmoor' bus to Postbridge. Alternatively, the moorland sections could be covered by means of several circular walks and ideas for these can be found in numerous books that are available about walks on Dartmoor. For various reasons you may wish to avoid the open moorland sections of the walk altogether, in which case we would suggest starting at Chagford and from there make your way to either Leigh Bridge (the confluence of the North and South Teign rivers) or to Chagford Bridge and start with Section 4 of the walk.

Note:- Before setting off from Postbridge you should bear in mind that there are no facilities en route for walkers until you get to Chagford (almost 11 miles). The first 7 miles of this are over open moorland and you should ensure that you are well prepared for any eventualities that could arise.

Postbridge

Despite its small size Postbridge is one of the best known and most visited places on Dartmoor. Throughout the year Postbridge for many is simply the start or end point of a good days walk, however the summer months bring a massive influx of visitors. The feature that attracts these visitors most is the delightful clapper bridge situated just downstream of the main road bridge. Although there are many clapper bridges on Dartmoor the one at Postbridge is the best known because of

The Clapper Bridge at Postbridge

its close proximity to the B3212. Despite their 'prehistoric' appearance clapper bridges, which are virtually unique to Dartmoor, only date back to when they were constructed by tin miners and farmers in the 13th and 14th Centuries. Spanning the East Dart River by means of three granite slabs supported on tall pillars, the bridge is one of the finest examples to be seen on Dartmoor. Before the clapper bridge was built the East Dart was crossed by means of stepping stones located just upstream from the more 'modern' road bridge built in the 1780's. The Dartmoor Information Centre by the main car park is open from Easter to the end of October Tel: (01822) 880272

13

1. POSTBRIDGE to GREY WETHERS

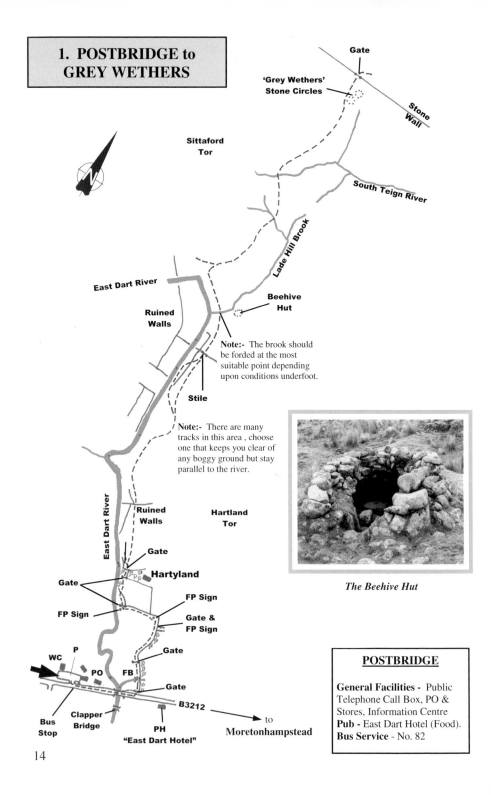

Gate

'Grey Wethers'
Stone Circles

Stone Wall

Sittaford
Tor

South Teign River

Lade Hill Brook

East Dart River

Beehive
Hut

Ruined
Walls

Note:- The brook should
be forded at the most
suitable point depending
upon conditions underfoot.

Stile

Note:- There are many
tracks in this area , choose
one that keeps you clear of
any boggy ground but stay
parallel to the river.

East Dart River

Ruined
Walls

Hartland
Tor

Gate

Hartyland

Gate

FP Sign

FP Sign

Gate &
FP Sign

P

WC

Gate

PO

FB

Gate

B3212

Bus
Stop

Clapper
Bridge

PH
"East Dart Hotel"

to
Moretonhampstead

The Beehive Hut

14

⟲ **From the Dartmoor Information Centre** in the main car park **go out to the B3212 road and turn left. Go along the road and cross over the East Dart River. Just after the bridge turn left to a small wooden gate** alongside a field gate. **Go through the gate onto a track and follow this track over Stannon Brook and then continue on to another gate.** After this gate the 'official' route follows the right-hand field boundary to the corner of the field and then goes left towards the river. Then as you near the river there is a gate on the right. However this route tends to be exceptionally muddy and as you are on open access land it may be easier to cut diagonally left across the field to the same gate. **Go through the gate and continue on by going alongside the river and through two more gates. As you go through the second gate,** with 'Hartyland' on the right, **you venture into open moorland surroundings** through which you will need to continue for another six miles or so until you reach the car park at Scorhill. **From the gate stay parallel and near to the river** as you go along the lower slopes of Hartland Tor **and continue on through an area of ruined walls.** In this area, as on much of Dartmoor, there are many tracks that can be followed but generally you should choose ones that avoid boggy areas but keep roughly parallel to the river. You should also be aware that many of the tracks in this area are flanked by waist-high gorse bushes, therefore the wearing of shorts may not be advisable! **Continue to follow the East Dart River to the next stone wall and cross this by means of an obvious stile.** After crossing this stile and continuing on you will eventually be opposite the valley from which the East Dart River has its beginnings. Close to here you will also come to the derelict Beehive Hut which serves as a useful landmark. This hut was constructed by tin miners as a place to store their tools whilst they took their tin to the nearest Stannary town to be weighed. The hut is located in a gulley about 80 yards up from where a brook known as the Lade Hill Brook joins the East Dart. **From the hut go down to the brook and cross it at a convenient point. Continue on by initially following a track that runs parallel to the East Dart River and then, after a short distance, bear right to continue along the lower slopes of Sittaford Tor** with the Lade Hill Brook now down to your right. **Keeping generally parallel to the brook follow the reasonably well defined path that crosses several watercourses along the way.** Up ahead of you trees marking the edge of Fernworthy Forest eventually come into view and then the outline of the Grey Wethers stone circles. The last 'stream' that you cross before reaching the stone circles is the humble beginnings of the South Teign River.

The Grey Wethers

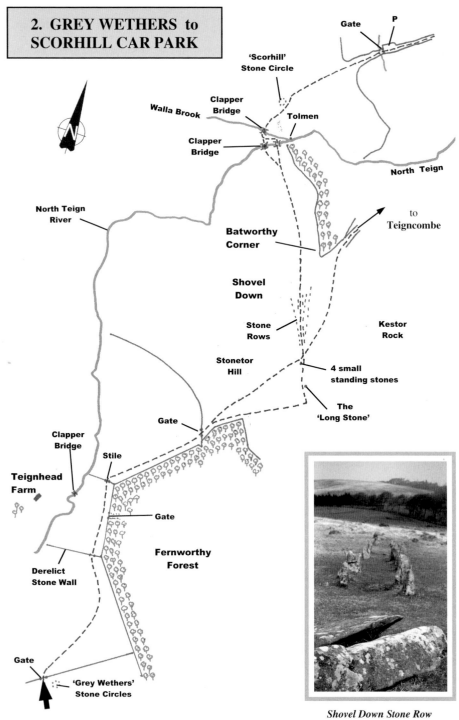

2. GREY WETHERS to SCORHILL CAR PARK

Gate P

'Scorhill' Stone Circle

Walla Brook

Clapper Bridge

Tolmen

Clapper Bridge

North Teign

North Teign River

Batworthy Corner

to Teigncombe

Shovel Down

Stone Rows

Kestor Rock

Stonetor Hill

4 small standing stones

Gate

The 'Long Stone'

Clapper Bridge

Stile

Teignhead Farm

Gate

Fernworthy Forest

Derelict Stone Wall

Gate

'Grey Wethers' Stone Circles

Shovel Down Stone Row

From the Grey Wethers continue to a gate in the dry stone wall ahead of you. **Go through this and then head diagonally right towards the stone walled edge of Fernworthy Forest. Keeping close to the wall follow it to a derelict stone wall. Go over this and continue towards the next boundary wall.** The river down to your left is the North Teign beyond which you will see a small tree lined enclosure which is the remains of Teignhead Farm. The farm which was once one of the remotest on Dartmoor was reached by means of the clapper bridge you can see a little further downstream. Before you reach the next boundary wall there is a gate in the wall you are following which provides a useful exit point off the moor should it become necessary. **When you come to the boundary wall cross over the stile and continue by keeping the forest edge on your right.** If you look ahead you will see the unmistakable flat-topped shape of Kestor Rock. This is your bearing if you wish to take the more direct route over Stonetor Hill after the next gate but you should bear in mind that the Tor will disappear from view as you drop down towards the gate. **Continue on down to the gate and go through.** You can now continue in the direction mentioned above or alternatively **continue by keeping the edge of the forest close to your right until you come to where the wall turns sharply away from you** to the right. **At this point carry on straight ahead for about ½ mile and then turn left onto a track going directly towards the 'Long Stone',** a tall standing boundary stone which you will see ahead of you. **From the stone continue ahead along the track.** On your left you will eventually see four small standing stones which, if you have followed the direct route over Stonetor Hill, is where the two routes converge again. **Continue straight ahead until you come to two sets of stone rows which go down in the general direction of Batworthy Corner.** The gate in the wall to the right of Batworthy Corner offers another exit off the moor that will take you direct to Teigncombe (in Section 3). **Where the stone rows diverge follow the left-hand row and continue on**

The Long Stone and Kestor Rock

keeping parallel to the stone wall on your right. Eventually you come to the North Teign which you cross by means of the Teign-e-ver clapper bridge. Continue on and cross another clapper bridge this time over the Walla Brook (see back cover photo). **From here head along a very well defined track to the Scorhill stone circle. From the stone circle,** the best preserved on Dartmoor, **head north-east uphill and then down to a gate at the end of a funnel shaped exit** which takes you off the moor and into the car park at Scorhill Farm.

3. SCORHILL CAR PARK to CHAGFORD BRIDGE

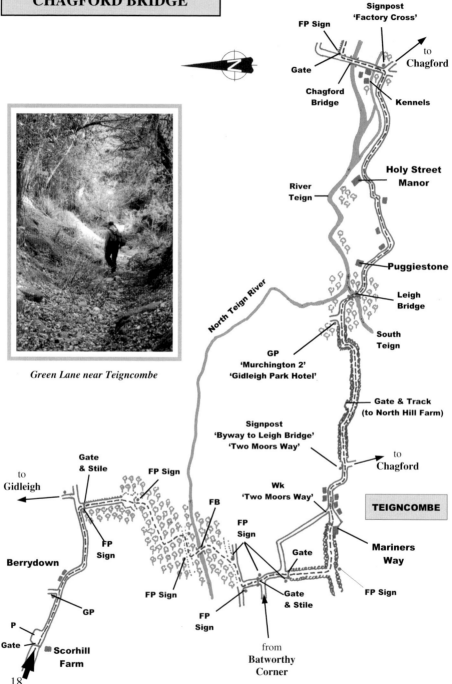

Green Lane near Teigncombe

Signpost
'Factory Cross'

FP Sign

to Chagford

Gate

Chagford Bridge

Kennels

Holy Street Manor

River Teign

Puggiestone

North Teign River

Leigh Bridge

South Teign

GP
'Murchington 2'
'Gidleigh Park Hotel'

Gate & Track
(to North Hill Farm)

Signpost
'Byway to Leigh Bridge'
'Two Moors Way'

Gate & Stile

FP Sign

to Gidleigh

to Chagford

Wk
'Two Moors Way'

FB

TEIGNCOMBE

FP Sign

Berrydown

FP Sign

Mariners Way

FP Sign

Gate

FP Sign

Gate & Stile

FP Sign

GP

Gate & Stile

P

FP Sign

Gate

Scorhill Farm

from
Batworthy
Corner

⬥ Go down the road as far as a T-junction and here bear right (signed 'Berrydown & Gidleigh ½ mile'). Continue on down the road, past 'Berrydown' on your left, and after almost ½ mile you will come to a wood on your right at the end of which there is a track leading into it. Over to your left at this point there is a fine view of Gidleigh with its Church and Castle. The track on the right is signed as 'The Mariner's Way' which you will now follow as far as Teigncombe. **Turn right onto this track and cross over a stile. Follow the track uphill to where it emerges into a clearing.** Ignoring the more obvious tracks ahead **bear slightly right to the signed path and follow this downhill into the wood** ('North Park'). **Continue to where the path joins a wider track** at a footpath sign. **Turn right** and after a short distance you will come to a footbridge on your left. **Cross the footbridge,** over the North Teign, **and then bear**

Footbridge over the North Teign

right to go along a path that climbs up through the wood ('South Park') **on the other side.** Near the top the path joins a wide track. **Here turn right and then take the signed lane on the left. Go up the short lane to a** gate and **stile. Cross the stile and go up the road until it turns to the left. Here go straight ahead through a gate and onto a signed track. Continue on this track until it meets yet another at a T-junction. Turn left and go down a delightful sunken lane and continue to where it meets a road** beside a bungalow on your right called 'Mariner's Way'. At this point you leave the route of the 'Mariner's Way', which goes off to the right, and will instead follow part of the 'Two Moors Way' (a brief description of the Two Moors Way appears on Page 22). **From the bungalow continue straight on down the road to a T-junction. Here go straight ahead and continue on until the lane takes a sharp right turn. At this point go straight ahead onto a byway** (signed 'Not suitable for motor vehicles', 'Leigh Bridge' and 'Two Moors Way'). **Continue on this byway until it meets a road** which to the left goes to the Gidleigh Park Hotel &

Holy Street Manor

Murchington. **Bear right onto the road and continue on to Leigh Bridge** which spans the South Teign. On the downstream side of the bridge you can see where the North Teign joins from the left thus combining to form the River Teign. **Continue on the road past 'Puggiestone'** which is named after a boundary stone that lies within the beautifully landscaped (but private) gardens, **and then past 'Holystreet Manor', until you come to 'Factory Cross'.**

If you wish to visit Chagford carry on straight ahead and the town centre is just under ½ mile away. Alternatively you can continue with the walk as far as Rushford Bridge in the next Section where another opportunity arises to walk into Chagford.

Chagford

Early Closing - Wednesday (but many shops remain open). *General Facilities* - Post Office, Banks, Hotels and B&B's, Shops, Restaurants, Cafes, Library and most facilities found in a compact moorland town. *Pubs* - The Globe Inn, The Three Crowns, The Bullers Arms and The Ring O'Bells, all of which serve food.. *Bus Services* - Nos. 173 and 179 depart from The Square. *Tourist Information* - The nearest information centre is at Moretonhampstead but information can be obtained on 01647 432571 or the parish website www.chagford-parish.co.uk.

Chagford, dwarfed by the bulk of Meldon Hill, was probably established in Saxon times and the name is thought to mean "the ford where the gorse grows". There are also many Bronze and Iron Age settlements on the nearby moors. In 1305 it became a Stannary town, one of four in Devon, where miners brought their tin for weighing, valuing and stamping. The old Stannary Court, which upheld the law and settled disputes, was situated on the site of the eight-sided Market House in the main square. The last tin mine in the area closed in 1903. The foundation stone of the Market House was laid in 1862 the original Stannary building having collapsed in 1617.

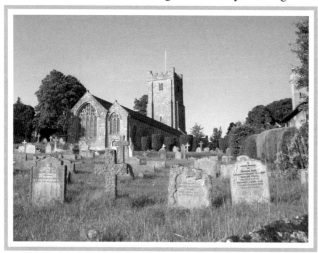

St Michael's Church Chagford

The structure of St Michael's Church mainly dates back to the 15th Century and but it was originally dedicated in 1261 by Bishop Branscombe, and some 13th Century work still survives. There is a small chapel in the church dedicated to St Katherine, the patron saint of tinners. Much of the woodwork in the church is by Edward Read of Exeter and the font was made by a local stonemason, John Aggett. In the granite floor of the sanctuary there is a memorial to Mary Whiddon who, it is said, was shot by a jealous former suitor as she left the church after her wedding in 1641. Whiddon House where she lived is now the Three Crowns Hotel and a short time later in 1643 Sydney Godolphin, a close advisor of King Charles, was killed there in a small skirmish between Royalists and Parliamentarians. In later years the hotel was patronised by the famous writer Charles Kingsley.

Endecott House, next to the Three Crowns, once housed the local school and is named after John Endecott, a Pilgrim Father, who later became governor of Massachusetts.

In the churchyard is the grave of James Perrott, a famous Dartmoor guide, who set up the first "Dartmoor letter-box" at Cranmere Pool in 1854. Dartmoor Letter-Boxing is a popular hobby in Devon and there are numerous books on the subject, which can be purchased locally, for anyone wanting to know more. There are good views from the churchyard over the Teign gorge to Castle Drogo. The War Memorial in the churchyard contains part of the old market cross.

One of Chagford's unique shopping experiences is the two side by side emporium's of James Bowden & Sons and Webber and Sons. Situated at the junction of Mill Street and the Square, both are family run and have been in existence for over 100 years. Webber's started as a saddlery and hardware business and Bowden's as an ironmongers. Bowden's contains a small museum to goods of the past. It is doubtful you will visit either shop without buying something and probably something you have been looking for for numerous years and have been unable to find! Up until the 1950's the town had its own Cinema, the Rex, in Store Street and has a thatched Bank, Lloyds, in the Square.

Bowdens (with Webbers to the left)

On the western outskirts of the town at Chagford Bridge (built around 1600) are the remains of the 19th Century woollen mill. This harnessed the power of the River Teign and was the largest employer in the area at the time, at its peak employing 1200 people producing blanket and serge. Cloth had been woven here since the 13th century. The mill leat by the bridge served a five metre undershot waterwheel. When the industry collapsed in the mid 19th century the site was taken over by George Hayter Hames. In 1866 he introduced modern sanitation to Chagford and established a Gas Works by the bridge, the latter proving uneconomic. In the 1890's part of the site was converted to use as a saw-mill but Hames also formed an electricity company with G. H. Read and generated hydro-electricity from the leat. This was used to provide street lighting in the town from late 1891, the first town west of London to have such an installation. Similar schemes were started locally using the power of the Teign including one to provide electricity for Castle Drogo.

For anyone wishing to obtain more detailed information on the town 'The Great Little Chagford Book' by Chips Barber will provide this.

The Market House

21

4. CHAGFORD BRIDGE to DOGMARSH BRIDGE

Kissing Gate

Dogmarsh Bridge

to Moretonhampstead

to Sandy Park

A382

Steps, Stile & FP Sign

FB

Mill End Hotel

SANDY PARK

Pub - The Sandy Park Inn (Food).
Bus Services - Nos. 173, 174, 179 and 671

Mill Leat

FP Sign 'Sandy Park'

Sculpture

Dogmarsh Wood

Gate & 2 FB's

Stepping Stones

Gate

Rushford Mill Farm

Swimming Pool

FP Sign

Rushford Bridge

Sculpture by Peter Randall - Page

FP Sign

FB

Gate

Gate & FP Sign

Gap in Hedge With FP Sign both sides

The Two Moors Way

The 'Two Moors Way' is just over 100 miles long and runs from Ivybridge on the southern edge of Dartmoor to Lynmouth on the north coast of Exmoor thus linking the two National Parks. The route covers a wonderful diversity of scenery, starting with some of the more remote stretches of Dartmoor and then on to the beautiful sections of the Dart Valley. It then climbs again before reaching the section of the walk you are now on. After passing through some delightfully unspoilt parts of central Devon, the route reaches Exmoor with its deep and wooded valley scenery and magnificent high moorland views. The path ends at the pretty resort of Lynmouth overlooking the Bristol Channel. An excellent guide book and accommodation list is produced by The Two Moors Way Association, "Coppins", The Poplars, Pinhoe, Exeter, EX4 9HH.

Gate & Stile

Weir

Gate

River Teign

Gate & 2 FB's

Riverdale Close

Gate

Mill Leat

Gate

Chagford Bridge

Gate & Kissing Gate

Gate & FP Sign

Downstream of Chagford Bridge

⬆ **Turn left at 'Factory Cross',** past buildings that contain remains of an old mill, **and cross over the old mill leat and then Chagford Bridge.** A short distance after you have crossed the bridge you will come to a gate and footpath sign on your right. **Go through the gate and then follow the path** between a fence and the river **to a kissing gate.** You will now walk alongside the river almost all of the way to Steps Bridge. **Go through the kissing gate and continue on** past some trees, with stone buttresses around them, **to a gate. Go through and continue,** initially with a stone wall on your left, **to another gate and then on to a footbridge, stile and another footbridge** that follow in quick succession. **From here continue on to a gate** into a wood. Notice the weir on your right. You will now walk alongside the mill leat that once fed Rushford Mill but that now supplies Chagford's outdoor swimming pool. **Continue through the wood to a small ford, gate and stile.** **Continue through the next two fields,** with trees on the right between the path and the mill leat, **by means of two gates.** At the second gate there is a footpath sign ('Chagford Bridge / Rushford Bridge and Withecombe') and to your right a footbridge over the mill leat. **Cross the footbridge and head diagonally right to a gap in the field boundary ahead of you. Go through the gap and head straight across the field** towards the river **to a gate** that takes you out onto the road.

This is where you have another opportunity to visit Chagford. To do so turn right to go over Rushford Bridge and the town centre is a further ¾ mile away.

⬆ **To continue the walk turn left and walk along the road and,** just after passing Chagford Swimming Pool on your right, **turn right at a footpath sign that directs you into the yard of 'Rushford Mill Farm'.** Notice the stepping stones that cross the river to your right. The path you are now on is known as 'The Fisherman's Path' and continues all the way to Fingle Bridge. **Continue straight ahead exiting the farmyard by a stile. Now follow the riverbank going through a gate and across two small footbridges and continuing to another gate. Go through this** and into 'Dogmarsh Wood'. Just after the gate look over to the small island in the river and you will see a small stone carving. This is the work of the famous sculptor Peter Randall-Page and is a good example of the split stone carvings for which he is renowned. **Continue through the wood bearing right at a footpath sign** ('Dogmarsh Bridge / Sandy Park'), **and cross a footbridge** which takes you out of the wood and into a field. **Go across the field to some stone steps and a stile onto the main road** (A382) **at Dogmarsh Bridge. Cross the road and go through a kissing gate** to rejoin the riverbank again.

23

5. DOGMARSH BRIDGE to FINGLE BRIDGE

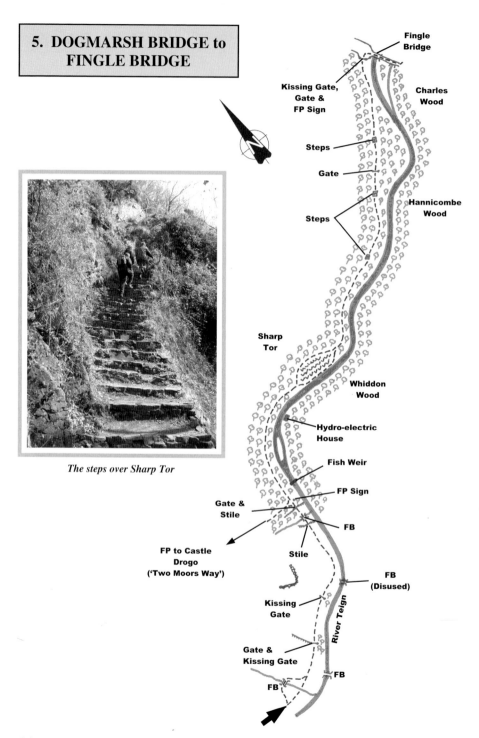

The steps over Sharp Tor

Fingle Bridge

Kissing Gate, Gate & FP Sign

Charles Wood

Steps

Gate

Hannicombe Wood

Steps

Sharp Tor

Whiddon Wood

Hydro-electric House

Fish Weir

FP Sign

Gate & Stile

FB

FP to Castle Drogo ('Two Moors Way')

Stile

FB (Disused)

Kissing Gate

River Teign

Gate & Kissing Gate

FB

FB

SECTION LENGTH = 2.26 miles

Continue on to a small footbridge (or shallow ford if the water level is low) **and then**, ignoring the footbridge over the river, **go through two fields by means of two kissing gates,** the second of which is in a non-existent field boundary, **until you come to a stile. Go over this and into the wood at Coombe and immediately cross a stone footbridge to another stile.**

At the footpath sign you now leave the 'Two Moors Way' unless you wish to visit Castle Drogo in which case turn left at the sign.

Castle Drogo

The property, owned by The National Trust since 1974, was designed by Sir Edwin Lutyens for Julius Drew a tea baron and founder of Home & Colonial Stores. Built between 1910 and 1930 it is the last 'castle' to be built in Britain. The granite structure is perched on a rocky crag some 900 feet above the Teign and is one of the most remarkable works that Lutyens ever completed. It combines all the splendours of a medieval castle with the comfort of the 20th Century. The gardens consist of medium size formal terraces with granite steps and walls. These are open all year round but the castle, shop, restaurant and tea rooms are only open at certain times from the end of March to December. Tel: 01647 433306 for details.

For the walk continue to follow the riverbank looking out for the fish weir which supplies the head water for the Castle Drogo Hydro-electric power house which you will see over on the other riverbank a short distance further on. Eventually you will come to a rock outcrop known as Sharp Tor and the steep steps that go up over it. If the river is low you can avoid the steps and walk around the base of the Tor but this is a rough and rocky route, which can be wet and slippery and should not be attempted in unsuitable footwear. **If the river is high follow the steep steps over Sharp Tor and then back down to rejoin the riverbank again** on the other side. The path now undulates alongside the river with steps every now and then at the more steeper sections. Eventually the footpath deviates away from the river before rejoining it again as you approach Fingle Bridge. **At Fingle Bridge go through the kissing gate out onto the road and turn right** towards the bridge itself.

The Teign near Fingle Bridge

25

6. FINGLE BRIDGE to HITCHCOMBE WOOD

Weir Mill

Weir

Hitchcombe Wood

Upperton Wood

Wooston Castle Hillfort

Fingle Bridge and Prestonbury Hillfort

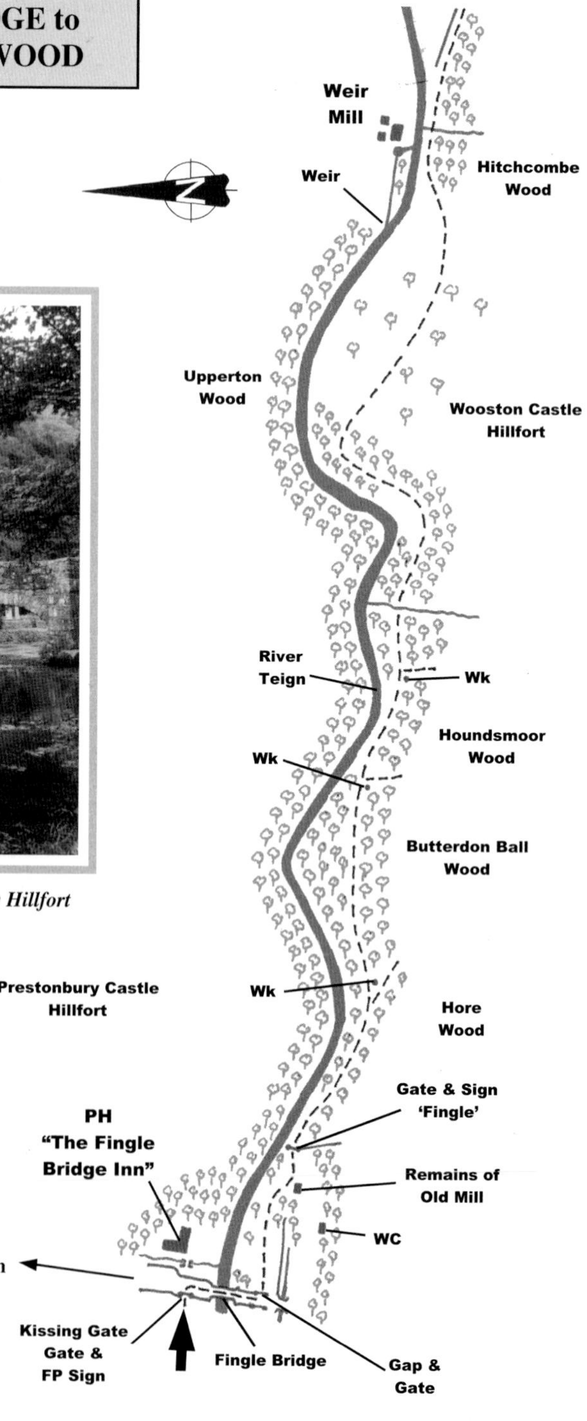

River Teign

Wk

Wk

Houndsmoor Wood

Butterdon Ball Wood

Prestonbury Castle Hillfort

Wk

Hore Wood

Gate & Sign 'Fingle'

PH "The Fingle Bridge Inn"

Remains of Old Mill

WC

to **Drewsteignton**

Kissing Gate
Gate & FP Sign

Fingle Bridge

Gap & Gate

Fingle Bridge and The Fingle Bridge Inn

Fingle Bridge Inn

Looking at it now it is hard to believe that the Inn, which until recently was known as 'The Angler's Rest', started life as a simple wooden hut from which cups of tea were served to travellers and fishermen. From this humble beginning back in 1897 the 'hut' has been progressively developed into the building that exists today. The combination of the pub and the old 16th Century packhorse bridge in such idyllic surroundings have made this one of the most frequented spots along the whole length of the Teign and you will be hard pressed not to pause your journey here for awhile. The Inn is open lunchtimes and evenings during the week but all day on Saturdays and Sundays. Tel: 01647 281287

Iron Age Hillforts

There three hillforts in this part of the Teign Valley; Cranbrook Castle on the southern side encloses an area of thirteen acres and is the largest of the three. The neighbouring hillfort of Prestonbury Castle lies about a mile to the north-east on the other side of the river and covers an area of four acres. Wooston Castle lies almost a further two miles to the east and like Cranbrook is on the southern side of the Teign. All three hillforts are accessible on foot and spectacular views make the effort very rewarding.

Cross over the bridge and turn left on the other side **through a gap by a gate and then continue by going through a field** alongside the river. When you come to the remains of the old mill **go over the depression that was the mill leat and bear left through a gate and onto a permissive path** (signed 'Fingle') which goes into a wood. **Continue through the wood on a substantial track** until you arrive at a point where the path splits at a waymarked post. **Here take the lower path and continue along the track** going past several more waymarks on the way. **Continue on this well defined track** through several more woods. Although the track itself remains fairly straight with waymarks every so often, the river occasionally meanders away from the track.

The walk towards Clifford Bridge

27

7. HITCHCOMBE WOOD to DUNSFORD MILL

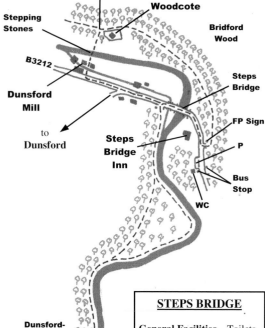

FP Sign
'Swanaford'
'Stepping Stones to Dunsford'

DUNSFORD

General Facilities - Public Telephone Call Box, PO & Stores
Pub - Royal Oak (Food).
Bus Service - No. 359

Woodcote

Stepping Stones

Bridford Wood

B3212

Steps Bridge

Dunsford Mill

FP Sign

to Dunsford

Steps Bridge Inn

P

Bus Stop

WC

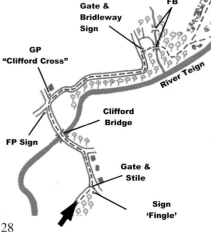

Stepping Stones at Dunsford Mill

Dunsford-Wood

STEPS BRIDGE

General Facilities – Toilets, Tea Room (summer only), Youth Hostel.
Bus services Nos 82 & 359

Gate & Bridleway Sign

FB

GP "Clifford Cross"

River Teign

Clifford Bridge

FP Sign

Gate & Stile

Sign 'Fingle'

Steps Bridge

⟲ As you approach the road near Clifford Bridge the track finishes at a gate and stile (signed 'Fingle'). **Turn left at the road and cross over the bridge and then continue up to Clifford Cross. At Clifford Cross take the road to the right,** signed to Dunsford, **and continue for almost ½ mile.** Eventually the road turns sharply to the left away from the river and a short distance after this there is a gate on the right, signed 'public Bridleway to Steps Bridge'. **Go through the gate and then over the first bridge** which crosses a stream **and follow the track back down towards the river again.** There are several paths and a bridleway going through Dunsford Wood which all eventually lead to Steps Bridge. One of the footpaths keeps fairly close to the river but this tends to get overgrown. By comparison the bridleway is wide and makes for easier walking. **Continue on through the wood until you come to the weir** just before Steps Bridge. **Follow a mill leat** on your right **and continue to a gap** by the end of the bridge parapet **and go through onto the main B3212 road.**

*You now have two alternatives; the 'Mill' Route or the 'Wood' Route. The 'Mill' Route is slightly shorter but involves walking along the busy B3212 road which has no footpath. You will also need to cross the Teign by means of stepping stones which is not for the faint hearted and should **NOT** be attempted if the river level is high or the river is running fast. Bear this in mind before making your choice, but we would recommend not using this route. However you will need to start out along the 'Mill' Route if you wish to visit Dunsford.*

The 'Mill' Route (and to visit Dunsford)

⟲ **Cross over the B3212 and turn left** (to face oncoming traffic). **Go along the road** past The Iron Mill with its large waterwheel. To visit Dunsford turn left at the road junction just after The Iron Mill. **Otherwise continue along the road** until you come to Dunsford Mill and at a FP Sign **turn right into the Mill grounds and go over a footbridge** spanning the mill leat. **Next cross the Teign by means of the stepping stones and then continue on a short distance to a surfaced track** upon which the 'Wood' Route joins from your right. **Turn left onto the track.**

The 'Wood' Route

⟲ **Turn right and go over Steps Bridge and follow the road around to the right and uphill.** Just past the Steps Bridge Inn (note this is not a public house as the name implies, and is closed in winter), you will see an opening in the wood on the left-hand side of the road. **Cross the road and go through the gap and then immediately turn left to go up a footpath** signed to 'Dunsford'. **Continue on this narrow path** through the wood which takes you high above the river. At one point there is an unsigned fork in the track, here **keep to the lower path** that eventually brings you out alongside a house called 'Woodcote' and onto a metalled track. **Turn right along the track** going away from the house **and continue on until you come to a triangular fork** where the 'Mill' Route joins from your left. **Continue straight ahead on the track.**

8. DUNSFORD MILL to LEIGH CROSS

Waybrook Cottage

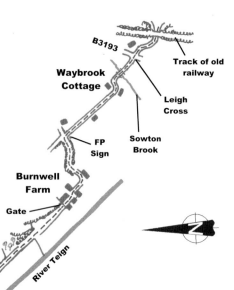

B3193

Track of old railway

Waybrook Cottage

Leigh Cross

FP Sign

Sowton Brook

Burnwell Farm

Gate

River Teign

Gate

FB

Gate & Cattle Grid

Sowton Mill

Gate

FP Sign

Sowton Cott Bridge

Gate & FP Sign

Swanaford House

Gate & FP Sign

Bramley

NT Sign 'Bridford Wood'

Sowton Mills

Continue on this track as it undulates alongside the river. Occasionally through the trees you can see the village of Dunsford over to your left. **Continue on the track to the end of the wood and then bear right with the track.** Follow it **between wooden fences until you come to the road** at 'Bramley'. **Turn left on the road** which immediately bears right. In a short distance it then bears left and then right again. Just after the entrance to 'Swanaford House' on your left (Note that this is called 'Swanford' on maps), **go through the wooden gate with "footpath" marked on it.** The signpost here directs you straight across the field. **Go across the field and down to a metal gate in the opposite corner of the field** which leads onto a track. **Turn right on the track and then immediately left at the road junction. Go down the road** until it joins the main road. **Carry straight on and go across Sowton Cott Bridge and then a minor one** over a mill leat. Where the main road goes round to the left, **turn right at a footpath sign onto a track. Go through a gate** or over a cattle grid **and continue down this track** with the mill leat on your right. **Go through the houses** keeping the first ones on your left and then the last one on your right **and continue down a path to a gate. Go through this gate and then** after a short distance **another gate, after which continue straight on ahead over a small stream** spanned by a footbridge with a sleeper top **and then through Beer Copse. Continue on the track until it comes to a metal gate** at 'Burnwell Farm'. **Go through the gate and into the farmyard and then bear left up the farm road** by a barn. **Where this joins a lane turn right and follow the lane down to the main road,** the B3193, **at Leigh Cross. Go straight across the B3193 and head towards a disused railway bridge.**

The Heathfield to Exeter (Teign Valley) Railway

The bridge up ahead of you once carried the Teign Valley Railway, the route of which you will generally follow and cross over in several places in the next few sections of this walk. The idea for a Teign Valley Railway was first conceived in 1862 as an offshoot of the line that ran from Moretonhampstead to Newton Abbot and which it was to join at Heathfield. However it was not until 9th October 1882 that the line actually opened and ran from Heathfield to Ashton with a mineral line forming an extension to Christow. The Exeter Railway, which effectively joined the line to Exeter, was opened on July 1st 1903 and became part of the Great Western Railway in 1923. Passenger services from Heathfield to Exeter ceased on 9th June 1958 and the demise of freight traffic gradually followed. The railway books mentioned in **Part 4** make interesting reading as well as containing many fine photographs of the railway and its surroundings.

31

9. LEIGH CROSS to DODDISCOMBSLEIGH

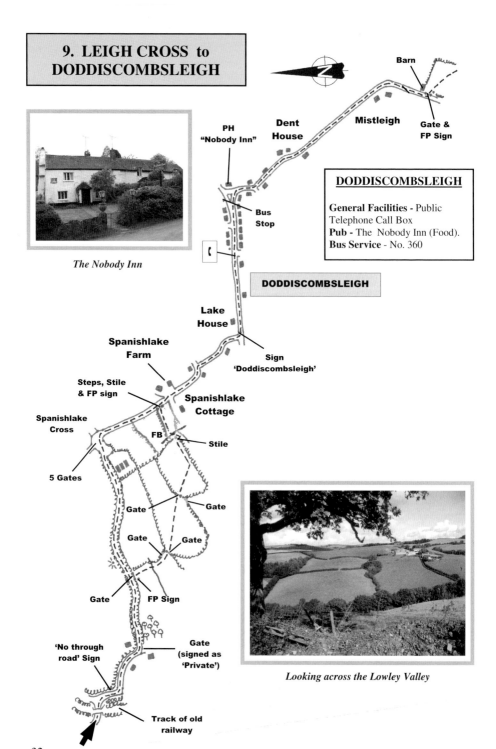

The Nobody Inn

Barn

Mistleigh

Gate & FP Sign

Dent House

PH "Nobody Inn"

DODDISCOMBSLEIGH

General Facilities - Public Telephone Call Box
Pub - The Nobody Inn (Food).
Bus Service - No. 360

Bus Stop

DODDISCOMBSLEIGH

Lake House

Spanishlake Farm

Sign 'Doddiscombsleigh'

Steps, Stile & FP sign

Spanishlake Cottage

Spanishlake Cross

FB

Stile

5 Gates

Gate

Gate

Gate

Gate

Gate

FP Sign

'No through road' Sign

Gate (signed as 'Private')

Looking across the Lowley Valley

Track of old railway

⟳ **Go under the railway bridge and turn right,** signed as a No Through Road, **and go along the road** until it bears left, and starts to go uphill. The metalled surface gives way to a green lane and becomes a steady uphill climb. Eventually you will come to a gate and FP sign on your right. If you are put off by what can be a very muddy area just inside the field you can continue on up the lane to a crossroads. Here turn right and go down the road until you see some steps and a footpath sign on your right which is where you rejoin the main route again. **Otherwise go through the gate and then keep close to the left-hand edge of the field. Continue on through a gap** by a stream **and on to two gates. Go through the right-hand gate and head diagonally down across the next field** towards two more gates in the far corner. This time **go through the left-hand gate and continue on the same bearing towards the hedge directly in front of you. When you reach the hedge turn left and go along the edge of the field to a stile. Cross over the stile and turn left** (your way onto a track is barred by a fence). **Cross over a footbridge and then keep close to a fence** on your left **to a stile. Cross over this to go down steps and onto the road. Turn right and go along the road** to a junction at 'Hereford Cottage'. **Here carry on straight ahead and until you come to a junction** with a more major road. **Turn left here and continue down the road past 'Lake House' and into Doddiscombsleigh.**

Doddiscombsleigh

Although this village consists of a delightful collection of whitewashed cottages, it is three buildings in particular that are worth mentioning. 'Town Barton' was the original manor house and is mentioned in the Domesday Book (1086). The house was the residence of Sir Ralph de Doddescomb from 1216 to 1272 and it was then that the village name changed from Legh Peverel to Doddiscombsleigh. Nearby is the 15th Century Church of St Michael which is the only one in Devon, apart from Exeter Cathedral, that still houses a complete set of five windows containing medieval glass. However it is the 'Nobody Inn', particularly renowned for its vast selection of whiskies and wines, which attracts most visitors to the village. The name itself has provoked much interest with many versions of how it originated. Built in the 16th Century the pub was originally a cottage which was used as a meeting place before becoming the 'New Inn' in 1637. It was still known as the New Inn in 1937 and it was not until 1952 that the name was changed to the 'No Body Inn'. The story goes that the name originated because after he died the innkeeper's body was unknowingly still in the Mortuary when the empty coffin was buried at his funeral service! Other tales abound but the above is probably the most plausible.

⟳ At the triangular War Memorial site the walking route bears round to the right past 'The Nobody Inn' (signed 'Ashton'), but if you wish to take a look at the Church and 'Town Barton', which are mentioned above, bear left at the memorial and they are just down the road on the right. **After bearing right at the war memorial you then bear left and go past 'Dent House' and continue down the road. Just after passing 'Mistleigh'** you come to a barn on the left just after which there is a metal gate, also on the left, with a footpath sign alongside it.

33

10. DODDISCOMBSLEIGH to RYDON (FARM)

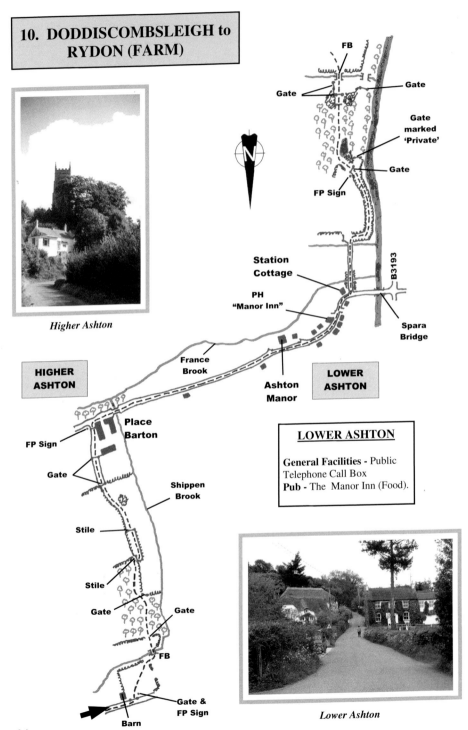

Higher Ashton

FB

Gate

Gate

Gate marked 'Private'

Gate

FP Sign

B3193

Station Cottage

PH "Manor Inn"

Spara Bridge

HIGHER ASHTON

France Brook

LOWER ASHTON

Ashton Manor

LOWER ASHTON

General Facilities - Public Telephone Call Box
Pub - The Manor Inn (Food).

FP Sign

Place Barton

Gate

Shippen Brook

Stile

Stile

Gate

Gate

FB

Gate & FP Sign

Barn

Lower Ashton

⬆ Go through the gate and head diagonally right down across the field. As you near the stream there are two gaps in the hedge on your right. **Head for the lower gap that is nearer the stream.** Go through and then turn left to cross the footbridge over the 'Shippen Brook'. **Turn right on the other side and go towards the gate** about 20 yds ahead of you which leads into a copse. **Go through this and onto a path** which goes through the copse. Go through the copse and as you come to a metal gate bear slightly left and continue to follow the path. In a short distance you come to a stile on your right. **Go over this and then turn left** into a fenced off part of a field. **Follow this to a stile** at the end **and then carry on along the left-hand side of the field until you come to a metal gate.** Go through this onto a lane **and then continue to another gate.** Go through this and into a farmyard. **Go down through the yard and out onto the road** at 'Place Barton'. **Turn right on the road** past Place Barton **and follow this road for about ¾ mile,** passing the entrance to 'Ashton Manor' on your left, **to Lower Ashton. Go past the 'Manor Inn'** on your left **and continue on until you cross the old railway.** The line of the old trackbed can be clearly seen in the gateway on your right. Immediately after passing 'Station Cottage' there is a narrow track leading off to the left. At this point the main road bears to the right to go up over Spara Bridge and it is worth sparing a few moments to make the short deviation to go and take a look at this old 16th Century packhorse bridge which spans the Teign. Returning to the walking route, **turn left after 'Station Cottage' to go along a track** which leads towards a field. **When you reach this turn right** towards the river **and follow the delightful path** which takes you along the tree-lined riverbank with the Teign gliding gently

Spara Bridge, Lower Ashton

alongside. This path can become extremely waterlogged in winter so be warned. Eventually you come out onto a broad track which is the old disused railway again. To the right of a footpath sign there is a gate on the old trackbed marked 'Private' which should be strictly respected despite the temptation to walk along the trackbed itself. **From the sign continue on through the wood** parallel to the trackbed and river until you come to a gate. **Go through the gate and then over the footbridge beyond it and into a field.**

35

11. RYDON (FARM) to FARLEY MILL

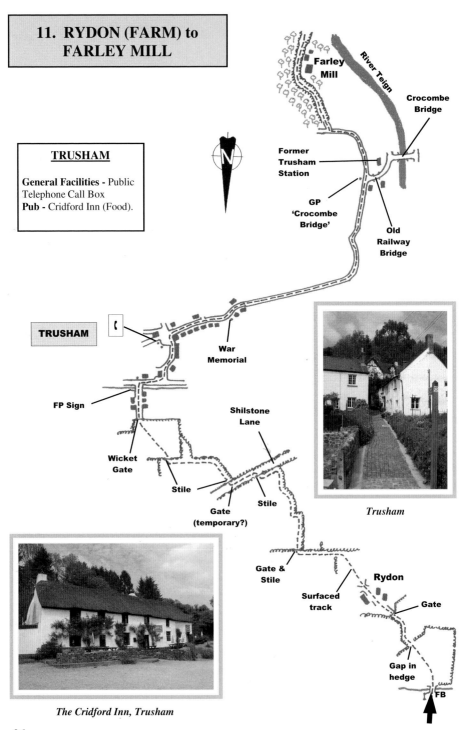

TRUSHAM

General Facilities - Public Telephone Call Box
Pub - Cridford Inn (Food).

Farley Mill

River Teign

Crocombe Bridge

Former Trusham Station

GP 'Crocombe Bridge'

Old Railway Bridge

TRUSHAM

War Memorial

FP Sign

Shilstone Lane

Wicket Gate

Stile

Gate (temporary?)

Stile

Trusham

Gate & Stile

Surfaced track

Rydon

Gate

Gap in hedge

FB

The Cridford Inn, Trusham

Bear left to go up the field, following the broad, grassy track that goes round slightly to the right of the hill, rather than the narrow path which goes straight up. **Go through a gap in the hedge and follow the track** keeping the hedgebank on your left **and continue on to a gate.** If you stop and turn around you get a magnificent view back across the valley from here. **Go through the gate and across the farmyard of 'Rydon',** with holiday cottages on your left, **and follow the track out on the other side of the yard. Go through a gap in the next hedge and continue to follow the track** along the right-hand side of the next field. About 150 yards after going through the gap you will find a gate and waymarked stile on your right. **Go over the stile into a field and then continue on** by keeping to the right-hand edge of the field. Here you will get another excellent view but this time by looking ahead of you. **Continue down to a stile** that takes you into a green lane ('Shilstone Lane'). **Turn left and then go through a gate** (note this gate may only be temporary) **and then right over a stile and into a field. Go through the field by keeping close to the right-hand edge** until you come to a stile in the far corner. You can now see Trusham ahead of you. **Cross over the stile and onto a path which you follow down the hill to a wicket gate. Go through the gate and then down steps** that take you between cottages before leading to a small footbridge. **Cross over this to reach the road.** If you require refreshments, the Cridford Inn is a very short distance up the road on your left.

Trusham

Trusham is made up of the idyllic combination of attractive cottages, a church and a thatched pub, set in a wooded valley with superb rural views all around the neighbourhood. The Church of St Michael's was erected in 1259 and completely restored in 1865.

Turn right and then immediately left into 'Rattle Street' (unsigned). **Go up the narrow lane and at the top turn right.** Go along the road passing the war memorial as you leave the village, **and continue on this road all the way down towards Crocombe Bridge.** Where the road bears right over the old railway bridge, signed 'Hennock', 'Chudleigh', **carry on along the road to the left** which passes alongside a building that was formerly Trusham Station. **Continue along this road and after about 300 yards, turn right** into Teign Lane (unsigned). **Go along this road and past Farley Mill**, on your right.

View upstream of Crocombe Bridge

37

12. FARLEY MILL to B3344 (CHUDLEIGH)

to Chudleigh

CHUDLEIGH

General Facilities - PO, Bank / Cash Machine (in supermarket), B&Bs, various shops inc Bakers, Chemist, Grocer, Chinese Takeaway, Fish & Chips, Public Telephone Call Box, WC.
Pubs - Bishop Lacey, Old Coaching House, White Hart, Ship Inn, Globe Inn (all serve Food).
Bus Services - Nos. 39 & 182.

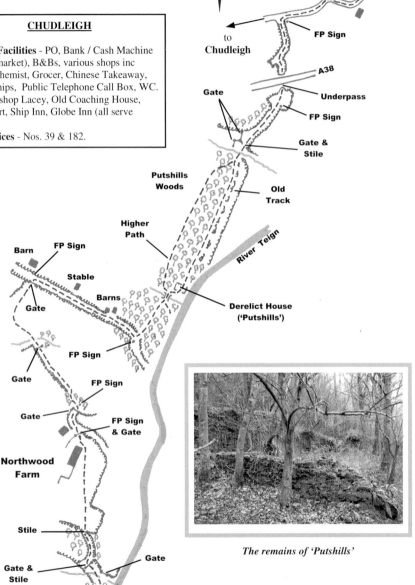

The remains of 'Putshills'

Continue on to where the track ends and crosses a stream. Here you will see a field gate immediately in front of you beyond which there is an obvious track across the field. **Do not go through this gate but instead bear left to a gate and stile. Cross over the stile and continue a short distance uphill to another stile.** (This last realigned section is a vast improvement on what used to be a permanently muddy and slippery slope). **Cross over the stile** into a field **and head diagonally left across the field towards the farm buildings** of 'Northwood'. **Go past the farm buildings to a gate and out onto a lane.** Go down the lane in front of the farmhouse **to another gate. Go through this gate and follow the signed path left up a sunken track** through the trees **for a short distance until you meet a farm track. Turn left on the track,** keeping the hedge on your left, **and follow it uphill and then down to a gate. Go through the gate, cross a stream and continue on the track** uphill until it bears round to the right **to a gate onto a lane. Turn right on the lane and go downhill and continue on to where the lane changes to a green lane** by the entrance to some stables. **Continue on this lane past two barns**, one new, one derelict. **As the lane gets steeper and starts to zig-zag look out for a gap on the left-hand side** which is marked with a footpath sign. **Take the footpath through the woods until you reach a stream. Cross over the stream,** by means of a plank footbridge. From here the public footpath goes left and up into the wood and continues at a higher level until rejoining the lower path at a stream crossing. The lower path is not a public footpath but is in regular use and is the more frequently used of the two. This lower path goes through the remains of 'Putshill' and runs parallel and to the left of an old sunken track. We leave the choice of route to you. As already mentioned the two paths meet again at a stream crossing and the remains of a stile. **Cross the stream and continue by following the obvious track ahead of you**. The track broadens out just before an underpass which carries the A38 dual carriageway. **Go through the underpass and uphill** past the sewage works entrance on your left. **Continue up the road** to its junction with 'Old Way' (unsigned).

If you wish to visit Chudleigh turn left here and the town centre is approx ¾ mile further on. Although there is another opportunity further on, this one is very much the quieter and less busy option.

Chudleigh
Unfortunately space does not permit an account of Chudleigh in this book but it is well worth a visit and offers the following facilities:- Public Toilets, Five Public Houses, Chinese Take Away, Fish & Chip Shop, Post Office, Lloyds TSB, Bakers, Chemist, Stores and Co-op Supermarket with a cashpoint machine

To continue the walk turn right and follow the road to its junction with the main B3344 road. At the junction turn left and go along the road until you come to 'Rocklands' on your left. (Straight ahead is your second opportunity to visit Chudleigh). **Cross the road to the junction on the opposite side.**

13. B3344 (CHUDLEIGH) to CHUDLEIGH KNIGHTON

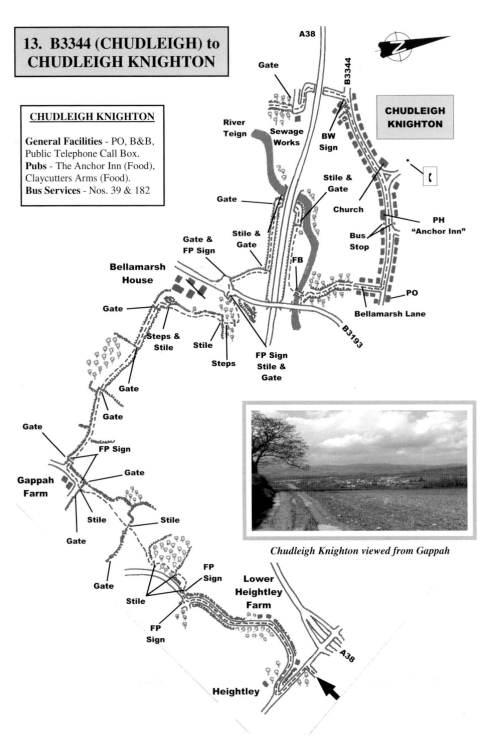

CHUDLEIGH KNIGHTON

General Facilities - PO, B&B, Public Telephone Call Box.
Pubs - The Anchor Inn (Food), Claycutters Arms (Food).
Bus Services - Nos. 39 & 182

A38

Gate

B3344

CHUDLEIGH KNIGHTON

River Teign

Sewage Works

BW Sign

Stile & Gate

Church

Gate

Bus Stop

PH "Anchor Inn"

Stile & Gate

Gate & FP Sign

Bellamarsh House

FB

PO

Gate

Steps & Stile

Stile

Steps

FP Sign Stile & Gate

Bellamarsh Lane

B3193

Gate

Gate

Gate

FP Sign

Gappah Farm

Gate

Stile

Stile

Gate

FP Sign

Gate

Stile

Lower Heightley Farm

FP Sign

Heightley

A38

Chudleigh Knighton viewed from Gappah

After crossing the B3344 to the road junction opposite, turn right and follow the road (which at one time was the main A38) **down past 'Heightley', and on to where it bends around to the left.** **Continue on this road** as it climbs past 'Lower Heightley Farm' and 'Bromfield' both on your right. When the road levels out look over to your left and you can see the imposing outline of Chudleigh Rock. **Continue on the road** and immediately after it takes a sharp turn right there is a stile (the footplank may be missing) in the right-hand hedge. **Go over the stile into a field and turn left to another stile.** **Cross this stile to go through Kiln Wood** before emerging from the wood soon after by means of another stile. **Head diagonally and slightly downhill across the field to a stile** which is hidden from view until you almost reach it. **Cross over this into the next field and head downhill and then up again to a stile** in the field boundary at the top. **Cross over this stile onto the road and turn right.** **Go along the road** until you see two gates and a footpath sign on your right. **Go through the gate immediately on your right and follow the well defined track** alongside the left-hand edge. Ahead of you is a superb view of Chudleigh Knighton and the Tors of Dartmoor beyond. **Go through the next gate** keeping the hedge on your left **to another gate.** **Go through this and continue on the track** with the hedge now on your right **to the next gate.** **Continue down** what is now a green lane **to another gate** shortly after which are some steps on your right leading up to a stile. **Cross over the stile into a field and continue on** keeping close to the fence on your left **to another stile.** **Cross over this and then go down some steps** and onto the open area at the bottom. **Turn left up to a gate and stile, crossing over the latter to reach the main road.** **Cross the road to the gate opposite and go through this** into the field **and onto a well defined track.** **Follow this track to a gate and stile** alongside the A38 **and then continue on towards the river.** **When you reach the river turn right** onto a concrete track **and go under the bridge. On the other side cross over a stile** on your right **and then go up the right-hand edge of the field** parallel to the A38. As the field narrows **go across to the footbridge and cross over the Teign** and into Bellamarsh Lane (unsigned). The initial narrow track soon widens out and becomes a surfaced road up to where it meets the B3344 in Chudleigh Knighton. **At the junction turn left and go along the road** into the village to the Anchor Inn. **Continue on downhill** towards the end of the village **crossing over what is known as 'Bunker's Bridge. After the bridge and housing estate roundabout turn left into 'Pipehouse Lane',** signed as a bridleway and 'No Through Road', **and go through the A38 underpass** ahead of you. The road turns left immediately after the underpass and then after a short distance it turns back on itself. At the bend and just after the entrance to the sewage works you will see a waymarked wooden gate on your left. **Go through the gate which takes you onto a green lane. Go along the lane,** ignoring several gaps on your left, until eventually it reaches an open area and bears slightly left towards the river. **At the river turn right and follow the footpath along the riverbank.**

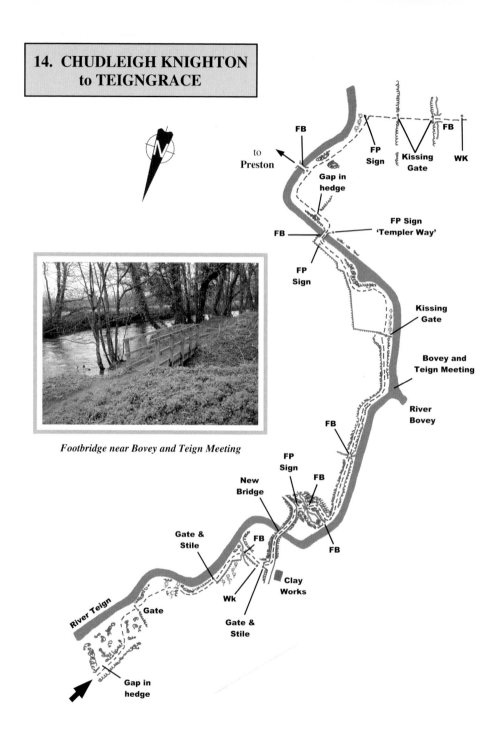

FB

to
Preston

FP
Sign

Kissing
Gate

FB

WK

Gap in
hedge

FP Sign
'Templer Way'

FB

FP
Sign

Kissing
Gate

Bovey and
Teign Meeting

River
Bovey

FB

Footbridge near Bovey and Teign Meeting

FP
Sign

FB

New
Bridge

Gate &
Stile

FB

FB

Clay
Works

Wk

River Teign

Gate

Gate &
Stile

Gap in
hedge

⚫ Follow the riverbank to a stile, alongside a small gate, and cross over into a field. Head straight across the field until the path meets the river again. Follow the riverbank until you come to another gate and stile. Cross over the stile and again continue to follow the riverbank until the footpath bears off to the right. Shortly you come to a footbridge beyond which is gate and stile leading onto the main road (B3344) opposite Newbridge Clay Works.

New Bridge

Turn left and go along the road, which can be fairly busy particularly with lorries, as far as a narrow hump-backed bridge. This is New Bridge. Cross over the bridge and, continue along the road for about a hundred yards to a footpath sign on your right. Turn right and go down to a footbridge. Cross over the bridge and go along the footpath with a mill leat on your right. Continue alongside the mill leat until you come to the river again. Turn left at a waymarked tree and go along the riverbank. You now follow the path alongside the river, crossing a footbridge on the way, for some considerable distance. Eventually you come to the appropriately named 'Bovey and Teign Meeting', the point where the Teign is joined by its largest tributary the River Bovey. Like the Teign the Bovey rises on Dartmoor and will be the subject of another book in the 'Walking Devon's Rivers' series. Continue on along the riverbank to a kissing gate leading into a field. Go into the field and go along the path keeping parallel with the river until you have to bear off left towards some scrub. The path eventually joins a track between the river and the clay works boundary. Continue on this track until you come to a footbridge. Go across the footbridge and turn left to go along the riverbank on the other side. You have now joined the 'Templer Way' which you will follow all the way to Shaldon. A brief description of this route is given on page 45. Go through a gap in the hedge and continue along the riverbank to another footbridge. Do not go over this but carry on along the path as it bears slightly away from the river to go through another gap in a hedge and then rejoins the river again. Continue along the riverbank to a signpost. Here you turn right to go across the field to a kissing gate. Go through into the next field and head straight for another kissing gate. Go through this and immediately over a footbridge, over a drainage ditch and cross the field towards a waymarked post.

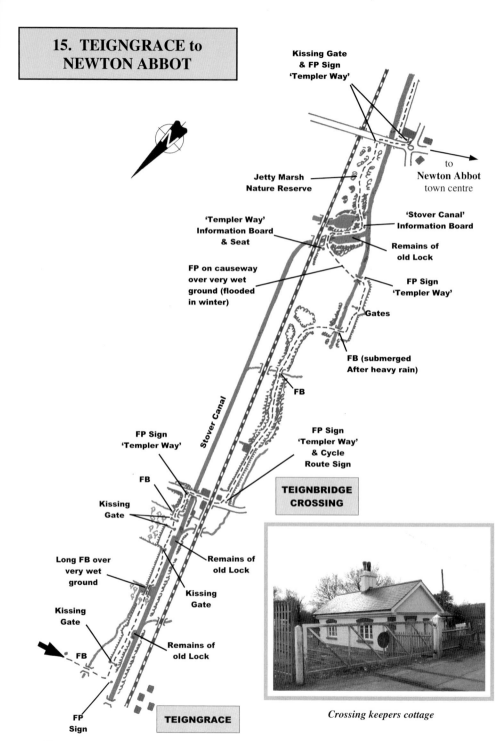

15. TEIGNGRACE to NEWTON ABBOT

Kissing Gate
& FP Sign
'Templer Way'

to
Newton Abbot
town centre

Jetty Marsh
Nature Reserve

'Templer Way'
Information Board
& Seat

'Stover Canal'
Information Board

Remains of
old Lock

FP on causeway
over very wet
ground (flooded
in winter)

FP Sign
'Templer Way'

Gates

FB (submerged
After heavy rain)

Stover Canal

FB

FP Sign
'Templer Way'

FP Sign
'Templer Way'
& Cycle
Route Sign

FB

**TEIGNBRIDGE
CROSSING**

Kissing
Gate

Long FB over
very wet
ground

Remains of
old Lock

Kissing
Gate

Kissing
Gate

Remains of
old Lock

FB

FP
Sign

TEIGNGRACE

Crossing keepers cottage

➋ **From the waymarked post go towards and cross over a footbridge and head towards the signpost ahead of you** which is on the bank of the now disused Stover Canal. At this point an alternative route of the 'Templer Way' joins from the right.

The 'Templer Way' is 18 miles long and links Haytor on Dartmoor to the sea at Teignmouth. Named after a local family the route closely follows the 'Haytor Granite Tramway' and the 'Stover Canal' the latter being built by John Templer and the former by his son George. Granite from the quarries at Haytor was used in the construction of London Bridge, The British Museum and the National Gallery. The route goes across a variety of terrain, ranging from open moorland, woodlands, field paths and tracks and finally, as on this walk, along the foreshore of the Teign Estuary.

At the signpost turn left to go through a kissing gate and then along the canal bank. Continue on the bank as far as a derelict lock. **From the lock continue on along the canal bank until you come to a series of footbridges** over a very wet area as a result of erosion of the canal bank. **Continue on between the canal and a post and wire fence** on your left **until you come to a kissing gate** by another derelict lock. **Go through and then over two stiles and a footbridge** soon after which you emerge on to main

One of several derelict locks on the Stover Canal

road at Teignbridge Crossing. **Turn right over the canal bridge and a level crossing and then turn immediately left after passing what was the old crossing keepers cottage.** You are now on a cycle route. **Go to the right of a wooden gate through some cycle 'slowing' posts and continue on along a surfaced track** with the railway on your left. Shortly after going over a footbridge the path bears away from the railway towards a chainlink fence. **At the fence bear left and continue along the path** which now goes between the fence and a stretch of water known as Whitelake. **Turn left over Whitelake by means of the sluice gate.** At this point you are at the stream's normal tidal limit. From the sluice you have entered into the Jetty Marsh Local Nature Reserve and **you should follow the path back towards the railway again. As you near the railway bear right over the remains of the old lock,** where the Stover Canal joined up with Whitelake, and then continue on to the old canal basin. **From here continue to follow the path through the reserve until you come to the main road** (B3195). **Go out onto the road and cross by means of the pedestrian crossing** near the roundabout. **Go back down onto the bank of Whitelake and the old canal via the metal kissing gate** on your left.

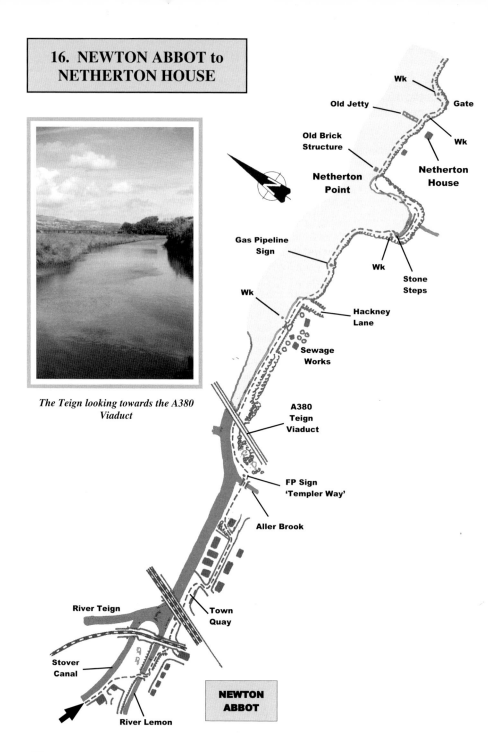

16. NEWTON ABBOT to NETHERTON HOUSE

The Teign looking towards the A380 Viaduct

Wk

Old Jetty

Gate

Old Brick Structure

Wk

Netherton Point

Netherton House

Gas Pipeline Sign

Wk

Wk

Stone Steps

Hackney Lane

Sewage Works

A380 Teign Viaduct

FP Sign 'Templer Way'

Aller Brook

River Teign

Town Quay

Stover Canal

NEWTON ABBOT

River Lemon

⬆ **Continue alongside the canal** until just before the railway bridge you come to a landscaped park area. **Bear right across the park to a footbridge. Cross over the footbridge** which takes you over the Teign's other main tributary, the River Lemon. The Lemon rises on Dartmoor near Haytor Rocks and a walk along this river will be described, along with one on the River Bovey, in another book in this series. **Go across the bridge and continue alongside the River Lemon and go under a railway bridge** (which carries the Heathfield branch which you have closely followed from Teigngrace). At this point the Lemon, and Whitelake slightly further upriver, enter the River Teign. **Continue on alongside what is now the Teign itself and go under another railway bridge** (carrying the main Newton Abbot to Exeter line) and out onto Town Quay. **At the end of the quay turn right up 'Forde Road'. Just after turning right turn left into what is also 'Forde Road' and continue along the road** until you see a signed path ('Templer Way' and 'Footpath') on the left which leads back to the river again. **Continue on this path alongside the river and go through some scrub** until you come to a footbridge. **Cross over what is the Aller Brook and turn left on the other side. Continue alongside the river, going under the A380 viaduct.** Eventually you come out onto the estuary foreshore.

As mentioned at the beginning of this book, and without wishing to be repetitive, it is still worth reiterating that the remainder of the walk from here to Shaldon should not be attempted without first checking the state of the tide. The remaining overall distance is 4 miles and as a general guide you should allow yourself approximately two hours either side of low water, particularly if you plan to stop along the way.

⬆ The remainder of the walk, until you near Shaldon, is along the estuary foreshore and therefore walking descriptions have not been considered necessary as the maps should hopefully indicate the various 'landmarks' along the remaining sections. So generally it is a matter of following the foreshore but being aware that in places the sand can be very soft and stones very slippery especially after the tide has just receded.

*One other word of warning:- **DO NOT ATTEMPT** to take short cuts across the inlets at Netherton Point (Section 16), Coombe Cellars and Arch Brook (both Section 17), as there is quicksand in these areas.*

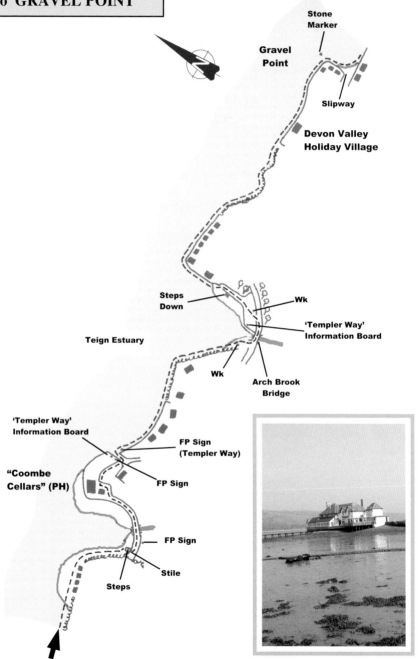

17. NETHERTON HOUSE to GRAVEL POINT

SECTION LENGTH = 2.06 miles

Stone Marker

Gravel Point

Slipway

Devon Valley Holiday Village

Steps Down

Wk

'Templer Way' Information Board

Teign Estuary

Wk

Arch Brook Bridge

'Templer Way' Information Board

FP Sign (Templer Way)

"Coombe Cellars" (PH)

FP Sign

FP Sign

Stile

Steps

Combe Cellars

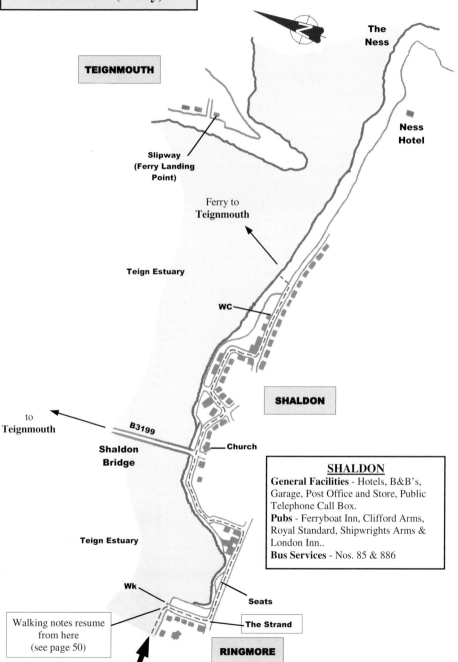

The Ness

TEIGNMOUTH

Ness Hotel

Slipway
(Ferry Landing
Point)

Ferry to
Teignmouth

Teign Estuary

WC

SHALDON

to
Teignmouth

B3199

Church

Shaldon
Bridge

SHALDON
General Facilities - Hotels, B&B's,
Garage, Post Office and Store, Public
Telephone Call Box.
Pubs - Ferryboat Inn, Clifford Arms,
Royal Standard, Shipwrights Arms &
London Inn..
Bus Services - Nos. 85 & 886

Teign Estuary

Wk

Seats

Walking notes resume
from here
(see page 50)

The Strand

RINGMORE

As you approach Shaldon you will see a waymark which guides you off the foreshore and onto a road. **Leave the foreshore and go up this road** ('The Strand') **and at the road junction turn left** along 'Ringmore Road'. **Continue along this road** passing an open area **until just past a castellated building where you turn left up a side lane** just before a letterbox in a wall. This side lane is signed with a 'Templar Way' waymark. **Continue on this lane until it joins the estuary** by a slipway **and then follow the path alongside the estuary to Shaldon Bridge. Cross the main (A379) road and go onto 'Albion Street'** which is between the Church and the estuary. **Continue along this road until just after it bears away from the estuary and turn left onto a road called 'Riverside'** which leads you back towards the estuary again. **At the slipway turn right on this road and follow it between houses until it bears round to the right and joins the main street** alongside a café. **Here turn left and go along the road until you come to the boarding point for the ferry to Teignmouth,** opposite the Ferryboat Inn. *Alternatively you can walk across the terrace at the rear of the café and along the beach to the ferry.*

AND THAT'S IT - JOURNEYS END, time to look around Shaldon or to take the short trip across the water to explore Teignmouth. The last half a mile or so of the walk from Shaldon Bridge is also part of the South West Coast Path.

The 'South West Coast Path' - Over the centuries, fishermen, coastguards and smugglers have contrived to create parts of this historic path. It is Britain's longest national trail and stretches for 630 miles through four counties from Minehead in Somerset right round the South West peninsula to Poole Harbour in Dorset. The path passes along some of the finest coastal scenery in Europe. With its enormous variety and contrast between bustling resort and quiet cove it is a never ceasing source of delight. The path is supported by the South West Coast Path Association, formed in 1973, whose aim is to secure completion of the path as well as its improvement and maintenance. The Association produce an annually updated guide book to the whole length. It contains information about accommodation, camp sites, youth hostels, ferries, tide tables and public transport. Enquiries and details of membership of the Association can be obtained from:- Liz Wallace, Windlestraw' Penquit, Ermington, Devon, PL21 0LU. E-mail *info@swcp.org.uk*.

Shaldon Bridge viewed from Shaldon

Shaldon

Shaldon is a picturesque village situated on the opposite side of the Teign Estuary from the very much larger town of Teignmouth. It is connected to Teignmouth by means of Shaldon Bridge which was originally built of wood in 1827 and at that time was the longest wooden bridge in the country. The road crossing over the bridge was at one time a toll road and

Shaldon

the Toll House can still be seen at the Teignmouth end of the bridge. The bridge has recently been strengthened to cope with the demands of today's traffic. Shaldon is also connected to Teignmouth by means of the ferry (foot passengers only) which has existed since the 13th Century and is reputed to be the longest continuously running ferry service in the country. Much of Shaldon's character lies in its narrow streets and alleyways all flanked by thatched cottages and Georgian houses. The village comes to life in the summer months especially when the regattas and annual water carnival are taking place. On Wednesdays in the summer the village green hosts a craft fair which is enhanced by the locals who dress up in Georgian costumes. As if to remind one of Shaldon's past, the local cove is accessed by means of the 'Smuggler's Tunnel' !

Teignmouth viewed from The Ness, Shaldon

PART 4
USEFUL INFORMATION

Information Centres

Postbridge	Car Park, Postbridge	01822 880272
Newton Abbot	6 Bridge House, Courtenay Street, Newton Abbot, TQ12 4QS	01626 215667
Shaldon	Car Park, Ness Drive, Shaldon	01626 873723
Teignmouth	The Den, Seafront, Teignmouth, TQ14 8BE	01626 215666
Moretonhampstead	Visitor Information Centre,	
	10 -11 The Square, Moretonhampstead.	01647 440043

District Councils

Teignbridge District Council	Forde House, Brunel Road, Newton Abbot, TQ12 4XX	01626 361101
West Devon Borough Council	Kilworthy Park, Drake Road, Tavistock, PL19 0BZ	01822 813600

Environment

MetOffice (South West)		0870 9000100
Weathercall	Devon and Cornwall	09068 505304
Environment Agency	General Enquiries	08708 506506
Environment Agency	Emergency for reporting environmental incidents	0800 807060
Teignmouth Harbour Master		01626 773165
Dartmoor National Park Authority, Poundsgate, Newton Abbot		01364 631303

Taxis

National Taxi Hotline		0800 654321
Chagford	John Chard	01647 433219
Chudleigh	Chudleigh Private Hire	01626 853129
	Chudleigh Cars on Call	01626 854748
Moretonhampstead	Aunt Sallys	01647 441143

Newton Abbot

1st Abba	01626 330011	1st Ace	01626 336444 / 336644
24hr Newton Abbot	01626 331221	1st A & A	01626 333999
1st Newton Abbot	01626 334000	A2B	01626 331236
Alansway	01626 363811	DM	01626 331007
Buddas	01626 334607	1st Jubilee	01626 200330
Churchill	01626 353656	1st Taxis	01626 330071
First A1	01626 331212	Fred Warren	01626 354569
Grange	01626 335580	Hills	01626 336680
Milber	01626 333500	Teignbridge	01626 367676
Paul Johns	01626 332222	Professional	01626 335151
Richards	01626 331661	Station	01626 330077 / 334488
Ray Pooley	01626 208837	Martins	01626 365814
John B's	01626 365373	Highweek	01626 204020
Abbot	01626 331717	Barrets	01626 211331

Teignmouth

Alpha	01626 773030
Jim's	01626 779079
Bryans	01626 776011
Steve Perry	01626 772599
Butch's	01626 779490
C Cabs	01626 778744

Public Transport (Enquiries)

Devon Bus	(www.devon.gov.uk/devonbus)	01392 382800
National Rail Enquiries	(www.nationalrail.co.uk)	08457 484950
National Bus Enquiry Line	(www.traveline.org.uk)	0870 6082608
National Express Coach Services		08705 808080
First in Devon & Cornwall	PO Box 141, Plymouth, PL4 6ZB	0845 6001420
Stagecoach Devon	Belgrave Road, Exeter, EX1 2LB (www.stagecoachbus.com)	01392 427711
	Regent Close, Torquay, TQ2 7AN	01803 664500
Alansway Coaches (Country Bus)	King Charles Business Park, Heathfield, Newton Abbot, TQ12 6UT	01626 833664
Town & Country Coaches	Riviera House, Milber Trading Estate, Newton Abbot, TQ12 4JD	01626 201052
Carmel Coaches	Carmel Garage, Station Rd, Northlew, Okehampton, EX20 3BN	01409 221237
First Great Western	(www.firstgreatwestern.co.uk)	0845 7000125 (Tickets)
South West Trains	(www.southwesttrains.co.uk)	0845 6000650 (Tickets)
Virgin Trains	(www.virgin.com/trains) 0870 7891234	0845 7222333 (Tickets)
Wessex Trains (Tickets)	(www.wessextrains.co.uk)	0870 9002320

Public Transport (Services)

The following services were available at the time of going to print but you should check the current status with the operator or council enquiry line as they are liable to change without much notice. Also not all services use the "route number" particularly the once a week and County Council supported services. Devon County Council issue regular area transport timetables which can be obtained from Tourist Information Centres or direct from the Council by calling 01392 382800.

No	Operator	Frequency	Route
12	Stagecoach Devon	Daily	Paignton-Torquay-**Newton Abbot**
39	Stagecoach Devon	Daily	Exeter-**Chudleigh-Chudleigh Knighton-** Bovey Tracey-**Newton Abbot**
82	First in Devon	Sat,Sun (Winter) Daily (Summer)	Exeter-**Steps Bridge**-Moretonhampstead-Princetown -Plymouth.
85	Stagecoach Devon	Daily	Exeter-Dawlish-**Teignmouth-Shaldon**-Torquay. (No service to Torquay on Winter Sundays)
85A	Stagecoach Devon	Daily	Exeter-Dawlish-**Teignmouth-Newton Abbot**.
173	Stagecoach Devon	Weekdays	Exeter-Drewsteignton-Castle Drogo-**Sandy Park Inn-Chagford**-Moretonhampstead-**Newton Abbot.**
174	Carmel Coaches	Sunday (Summer only)	Okehampton-Drewsteignton-Castle Drogo-**Sandy Park Inn** - Moretonhampstead-Bovey Tracey-Widecombe.
179	First in Devon	Weekdays	Okehampton-**Sandy Park-Chagford**-Moretonhampstead.
182	Country Bus	Weekdays	**Newton Abbot-Chudleigh Knighton-Chudleigh.**
184	Country Bus	Weekdays	**Newton Abbot**-Bishopsteignton-**Teignmouth.**
193	Town & Country	Wed & Fri	**Newton Abbot-Teigngrace**-Haytor.
359	Stagecoach Devon	Weekdays	Exeter-**Dunsford-Steps Bridge**-Moretonhampstead.
360	Stagecoach Devon	Weekdays	Exeter-**Doddiscombeleigh- Teign House Inn-** Christow.
361	Country Bus	Wed & Sat	Christow-**Ashton Bridge**-Trusham Cross-**Newton Abbot.**
671	Carmel Coaches	Wed only	Okehampton-**Chagford**-Moretonhampstead-**Newton Abbot.**
886	Country Bus	Wed & Fri	**Newton Abbot-Combeinteignhead-Shaldon-**

Teignmouth.

N2	Country Bus	Sat Evenings	Dawlish-**Teignmouth-Shaldon**-Torquay.

South West Trains, First Great Western & Wessex Trains   Serve Teignmouth & Newton Abbot Stations
Daily
Virgin Trains   Serve Newton Abbot Station Daily

Accommodation
This being a tourist area there are numerous accommodation possibilities and rather than list a selection we suggest that you contact the local Tourist Information Centres for more details.

Public Houses
Below is a list of public houses passed on the walk or are within half a mile of the walking route.

Chagford	Globe Inn	01647 433485
	Ring O' Bells	01647 432468
	Three Crowns	01647 433444
	Buller Arms	01647 432348
Sandy Park	Sandy Park Inn	01647 432236
Fingle Bridge	Fingle Bridge Inn	01647 281287
Dunsford	Royal Oak	01647 252256
Christow Bridge	Teign House Inn	01647 252286
Doddiscombsleigh	Nobody Inn	01647 252394
Lower Ashton	Manor Inn	01647 252304
Trusham	Cridford Inn	01626 853694
Chudleigh	(See Section 12)	
Chudleigh Knighton	Claycutters Arms	01626 853345
	Anchor Inn	01626 853213
Newton Abbot	None passed directly but there are numerous in the town.	
Combeinteignhead	Combe Cellars	01626 872423
Shaldon	Clifford Arms	01626 872311
	Ferryboat Inn	01626 872340
	Royal Standard	01626 872442
	Shipwrights Arms	01626 873237
	London Inn	01626 872453

Other Notes

Steps Bridge (Section 7)	Although called the 'Steps Bridge Inn' it is in fact a Restaurant and Tea Room and is open on certain summer days only.

BIBLIOGRAPHY

The following books were either useful sources of reference or make recommended reading. With so many books available the list is not intended to be definitive, but merely a small selection of those we came across during our research.

HOSKINS, W.G.	*DEVON.*	DAVID & CHARLES, 1972
PAGE, J.L.W.	*THE RIVERS OF DEVON.*	SEELEY AND CO.LTD, 1893
WILLS, G.	*DEVON ESTUARIES.*	DEVON BOOKS, 1992
GRIFFITHS,G.	*HISTORY OF TEIGNMOUTH*	EX LIBRIS PRESS, 1989
JONES, R	*A BOOK OF NEWTON ABBOT*	EX LIBRIS PRESS, 1986
SALE, R.	*RAMBLER'S GUIDE - DARTMOOR*	HARPERCOLLINS, 2000
BEAVIS, D.	*THE TEMPLER WAY*	DEVONSHIRE PRESS, 1996
POMROY, L.W.	*HEATHFIELD TO EXETER RAILWAY*	ARK PUBLICATIONS, 1995
MITCHELL, V.	*BRANCH LINE TO*	
& SMITH, K.	*MORETONHAMPSTEAD*	MIDDLETON PRESS, 1998
BARBER, C.	*GREAT LITTLE CHAGFORD BOOK*	OBELISK PUBLISHING, 1997

Have you read the other two books in the "WALKING DEVON'S RIVERS" series ?

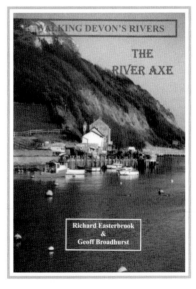

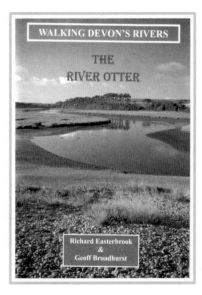

The River Axe
ISBN: 0 9538272 0 8
Price £3.95

The River Otter
ISBN: 0 9538272 1 6
Price £4.95

These may both be purchased direct from Easterhurst Publications Ltd
(address on Page 2)

YOUR WALK RECORD

Use this page to record the dates on which you completed each section

Section No	Length (miles)	Date completed and Notes
1	3.18	
2	3.95	
3	3.74	
4	1.83	
5	2.26	
6	2.21	
7	3.46	
8	2.11	
9	2.29	
10	2.03	
11	2.30	
12	2.28	
13	2.69	
14	2.95	
15	1.76	
16	2.36	
17	2.06	
18	0.95	

Total   44.41 miles